Lovely Lacy Knits

Eva-Maria Maier

D1717118

0 11557 01479 2

Contents

Introduction

In this book, I would like to introduce you to my passion for knitting, which has been nurtured by my mom since I was very young. Expect uncommon knit designs, richly embellished with ribbons, fabric, and beads. Waiting for you, too, are crocheted and sewn edgings and adornments, bound to become favorites! The main idea is to adorn oneself with beauty and to discover new creative ways. I want to inspire you to play with color nuances and to explore the vast riches of your fiber treasure collection. Develop your very personal style by combining antique little bits from Grandma's sewing basket with an array of contemporary materials.

Special thanks to my wonderful family for supporting me in this endeavor: First of all to Felix for his cooking magic, and to my parents, particularly my mom, ever so full of ideas, as well as to my father-in-law with his impressive arsenal of precious antiques.

Kind regards,
Eva

Lace
Sampler Scarf

Six pretty lace patterns lend this scarf
an elegant flair.

Finished Measurements

75 x 14 in./190 x 35 cm

Yarn

Light weight #3 linen/rayon/cotton blend yarn (shown in Permin
Scarlet; 58% linen, 26% rayon, 16% cotton; 164 yd./150 m per 1.8
oz./50 g skein; Powder Pink and Natural)
- 656 yd./600 m light pink
- 164 yd./150 m off-white

Needles and Other Materials

- US 6 (4 mm) straight needles
- US C-2 (2.75 mm) or D-3 (3.25 mm) crochet hook
- Printable silk fabric, 3 x 4.24 in./7.5 x 10.5 cm (includes seam
  allowance)
- Solid-colored off-white/natural cotton fabric, 6.75 x 6.25 in./17 x
  16 cm
- Pink seed beads
- Small pearl bead
- 14 in./35.5 cm cream bobbin lace
- 10 in./25.5 cm pastel pink ribbon
- 1.3 in./3.3 cm pastel pink flower-shaped button
- Sewing machine
- Color printer
- Sewing needle
- Iron

Gauge

19 sts in garter st = 4 in./10 cm (gauge is not critical for this project)

Notes

- Each chart is worked immediately after the previous chart; there are
  no rows between charts.
- The scarf is bordered by garter stitch edging. The number of edge
  stitches (at beginning of row, after the selvedge stitch and before the
  charted repeats; at end of row, after the charted repeats and before
  the slipped selvedge stitches) varies from stitch pattern to stitch pattern. Work the exact number of edging stitches and pattern repeats
  as indicated for each individual stitch pattern.
- Maintain selvedge stitches throughout: Knit through the back loop
  first stitch of row, slip last stitch of row knit-wise.

Scarf

With pink, cast on 67 sts and work 7 rows in garter stitch.

Work Chart 1 for 14 in./35 cm, as follows: The pattern repeat is 8
  sts wide. K1-tbl, k4, work "Begin" (8 sts wide) once, work pattern
  repeat (8 sts wide) 6 times (48 sts), k4, sl1 k-wise.

Work Chart 2 for 10 in./25 cm, as follows: The pattern repeat is 6
  sts wide. K1-tbl, K5, work pattern repeat 9 times (54 sts), k6, sl1
  k-wise. End with a RS row (Row 3).

Work Chart 3 for 4 in./10 cm, as follows: The pattern repeat is 2 sts
  wide. K1-tbl, k5, work pattern repeat 27 times (54 sts), k6, sl1
  k-wise.

Work Chart 4 for for 27.5 in./70 cm, as follows: The pattern repeat
  is 11 sts wide. K1-tbl, k5, work pattern repeat 5 times (55 sts), k5,
  sl1 k-wise.

Work Chart 5 for 7 in./18 cm, as follows: The pattern repeat is 6
  sts wide. K1-tbl, k5, work pattern repeat 9 times (54 sts), k6, s1
  k-wise.

Work Chart 6 for 4.75 in./12 cm, as follows: The pattern repeat is 8
  sts wide. K1-tbl, k4, work pattern repeat 7 times (56 sts), k4, sl1
  k-wise.

Work in garter stitch for 7 rows and bind off.

Weave in all ends.

Edging

With off-white, work crocheted picot edging into every other stitch
  (of the selvedge and bound off sts) around, as follows.

Set-up: Work 1 single crochet to attach the working yarn to the edge
  of the fabric.

Step 1: Work 3 chain stitches.

Step 2: Work a single crochet into the third chain from the hook,
  yarn over and pull the yarn through the chain and through the
  loop on the hook.

Repeat these two steps around, working into every other stitch.

In wrong side rows, purl all stitches. (Except for chart 3.)

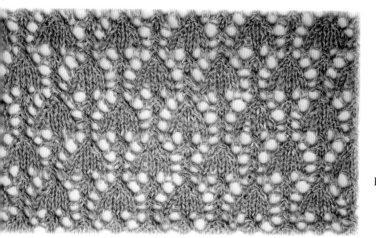

Chart 1 —
Staggered Tulip Pattern

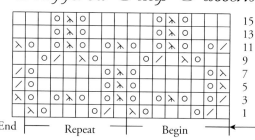

End | Repeat | Begin

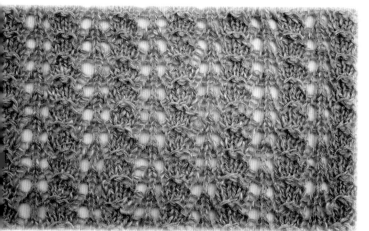

Chart 2 —
Fan Pattern

o	−	⋏	−	o		3
						1

Chart 3 —
Bobble Pattern

The stitch pattern is created in WS rows to appear on RS of fabric.

V	⋏	3
⋏	V	1

☐	knit
−	purl
o	yarn over
⋏	sk2p (sl1, k2tog, psso)
⋋	skp (sl1, k1, psso)

In wrong side rows, purl all stitches.

Chart 4 — Wave Pattern

∧	∧	ο		ο		ο		ο	∧	∧	3
											1

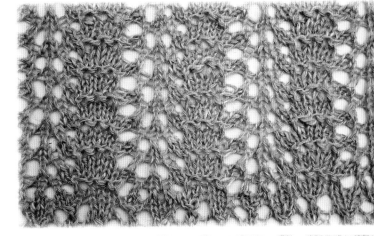

Chart 5 — Rosebud Pattern

ο	⋏	ο			3
		ο	⋏	ο	1

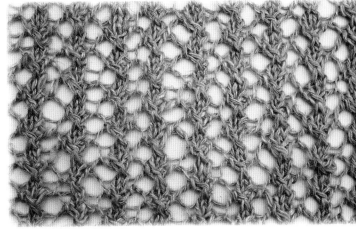

Chart 6 — Tulip Pattern

	ο	⋏	ο		ο	⋏	ο	7
ο	/		⋏	ο				5
				ο	⋏	ο		3
				ο	⋏	ο		1

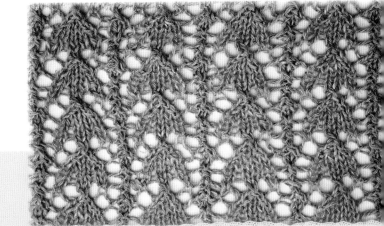

/	k2tog
⋏	p3tog
∧	p2tog
⋁	3 from 1 ([k1, yo, k1] into the same st)

Pocket

Print angel motif (below) onto printable fabric and cut it out with sufficient seam allowance, which is already included in the 3 x 4.25 in./7.5 x 10.5 cm size. Before printing, arrange as many motifs as will fit onto one sheet of printable fabric. After printing, iron fabric from the wrong side.

Fold cotton fabric, wrong sides facing inwards, into a 6.75 x 3.25 in./17 x 8 cm rectangle and sew on angel motif.

Sew ribbon onto upper fabric fold line, forming a button loop from the ribbon in the center.

Sew the pocket to the middle of the scarf's garter stitch section, folding the seam allowance under at the sides.

Sew bobbin lace along the whole width of the scarf and at the bottom edge of the pocket as well.

Decorate the pocket with beads. Sew the button onto the scarf. Carefully block the scarf into shape.

Printing Motifs to Printable Fabric

Scan the illustration from the book (or another of your choosing) using a standard scanner, preferably at a resolution of 300 dpi, to a scale of 1:1 (do not enlarge or reduce in size). You may also use copyright-free images available on the Internet.

Printable fabric is suitable for inkjet printers only. Place a sheet of fabric into the printer, select fabric characteristics and orientation according to the material chosen. The sample shown in the pictures used a piece of fabric 8.5 x 11 in. It is important to uncheck the "fit to page size" option so that the illustration won't get enlarged or reduced. Now, print the picture onto the fabric, and allow it enough time for proper drying afterward before handling. Remove the paper backing and rinse the fabric under running water until the water stays clear and no more excess dye is being washed out. Let the fabric dry thoroughly and iron it carefully from the wrong side before proceeding according to instructions.

Note: Color differences are unavoidable, owing to different printer models by various manufacturers as well as user-defined settings in the printer menu.

Template

Delicate Shoulder Wrap

This delicate and beautiful knit shawl gently embraces the shoulders.

Measurements

Circumference: 44 in./112 cm around at widest point in bulky yarn

Yarn

Bulky weight #5 wool/linen yarn (shown in Permin Carmen; 85% wool, 15% linen; 55 yd./50 m per 1.8 oz./50 g skein; Red)
- 220 yd./200 m red

Lace weight #0 mohair/silk yarn (shown in Permin Angel; 70% kid mohair, 30% silk; 230 yd./210 m per 0.9 oz./25 g skein; Cream and Red)
- 230 yd./210 m off-white
- 230 yd./210 m red

Needles and Other Materials

- US 15 (10 mm) circular knitting needle, 16 in./40 cm long
- US 15 (10 mm) circular knitting needle, 24 in./60 cm long
- US 8 (5 mm) circular knitting needle, 32 in./81 cm long
- US B-1 (2.25 mm) or C-2 (2.75 mm) crochet hook
- Tapestry needle
- Steam iron or clothes steamer

Gauge

10 sts in St st with bulky weight yarn = 4 in./10 cm

Notes

- The shoulder wrap is started at the collar and worked downward in the round.

Shoulder and Chest Section

Using 16 in./40 cm US 15 circular needle and bulky weight yarn, cast on 60 sts.

Join into round and work in [k2, p2] ribbing for 12 in./30 cm.

Work in St st for 5 rounds, then purl 1 round.

Change to 24 in./60 cm US size 15 circular needle.

*Knit 1 round, evenly distributing 10 M1 increases (see page 56 for how to Make 1).

Work in St st for 4 rounds, then purl 1 round.

Repeat from * 4 times for a total of 110 sts on the needles.

Knit 1 final round, but don't bind off.

Red Ruffle

Using 32 in./81 cm US 8 circular knitting needle and red lace weight yarn, make 6 from 1 by working [k1, p1] 3 times into every stitch of the previous round for a grand total of 660 sts.

Work in St st for 6 rounds, then bind off all sts.

White Lace

Beginning at the last knit round in the bulky yarn, with wrong side facing and white lace weight yarn, use crochet hook to make 4 from 1 by working [k1, yo, k1, yo] into each stitch, placing the new sts and yo's onto your knitting needle.

Work in St st for 3 rounds, then continue with charted stitch pattern, repeating Rounds 1–2 six times, then continuing with row 13 in chart.

Bind off stitches with crochet hook according to crochet chart, in alternating groups of 3 and 5 sts with chain arcs of ch9 in between, repeating around until all sts are bound off.

Weave in all ends.

Gently steam block the lace edging of the shawl.

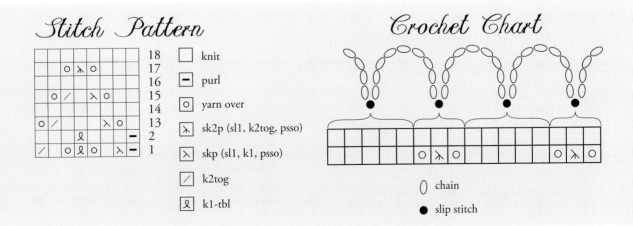

Stitch Pattern

		○	人	○			18 / 17
	○	/		人	○		16 / 15
○	/				人	○	14 / 13
			ℓ			—	2
/		○	ℓ	○	人	—	1

- ☐ knit
- ⊟ purl
- ○ yarn over
- 人 sk2p (sl1, k2tog, psso)
- ⅄ skp (sl1, k1, psso)
- ╱ k2tog
- ℓ k1-tbl

Crochet Chart

- ◯ chain
- ● slip stitch

Comfort Socks

Pamper your feet with cozy socks embellished
with ribbons and beads.

Measurements

Leg Circumference: 8.5 in./21.5 cm, unstretched

Yarn

Super fine weight #1 sock yarn (shown in Permin BabySock; 80% wool, 20% polyamide; 230 yd./210 m per 1.8 oz./50 g skein; Grey-Tan)

- 230 yd./210 m gray-tan

Needles and Other Materials

- US 1.5 (2.5 mm) set of double-pointed needles
- Stitch holder or waste yarn
- Tapestry needle
- Small dark silver-gold metallic beads
- Fine needle for threading beads
- 4 in./10 cm woven jacquard ribbon with red flowers
- 16 in./40.5 cm woven jacquard ribbon with leafing vine
- Glue for pre-threading beads (to make a point at tip of yarn for stringing)

Gauge

30 sts in St st = 4 in./10 cm

Special Stitch

K1 with Bead: Knit 1, slipping a bead to the outer portion of the knitted fabric before completing the stitch.

Leg

Pre-thread 56 beads onto sock yarn.

Cast on 64 sts, divide evenly on 4 DPNs, and join to work in the round.

Round 1: K6, *p2, k2; rep from * around.

Round 2: K6, *p2, k1, k1 with bead; rep from * around.

Round 3: K6, *p2, k2; rep from * around.

Round 4: K6, *p2, k1 with bead, k1; rep from * around.

Rounds 5–11: K6, *p2, k2; rep from * around.

Rounds 12–14: Rep Rounds 2–4.

Rounds 15–16: K6, *p2, k2; rep from * around.

From Round 17 onward: K6, p2, work Tulip Pattern over 27 sts, p2, k25, p2. Work 6 repeats of Rounds 1–8 of the Tulip Pattern Chart.

Place the 32 upper foot sts on hold, using a stitch holder or a piece of waste yarn.

Heel and Gusset

Transfer all 32 heel sts together on one DPN and work the heel flap in back and forth rows.

For the heel flap, work in St st (k on RS, p on WS) over the sts marked "heel" in the chart for 30 rows (2.5 in./6 cm). For selvedge sts, slip the first and k the last st of every row.

To turn the heel, in the following RS row: K1-tbl, k20, k2tog-tbl, k1. Turn work.

WS: Sl1, p11, p2tog, p1. Turn work.

RS: Sl1, k11, k2tog-tbl, k1. Turn work.

Repeat last WS and RS rows until 12 sts are left from the 32 heel sts. (The last 2 rows will end with k2tog or p2tog.)

Prepare to work in the round again. Place the sts for the upper foot back onto needles and pick up and knit 16 gusset sts from the selvedge at either side of the heel flap. Continue to work in pattern, working Rows 1–8 from chart 2 times, while at the same time decreasing, as follows: k2tog at the beginning of the heel sts and skp the last 2 heel sts, until 64 sts are left.

Foot

For the upper foot, work 2 pattern repeats of the Tulip Pattern (Chart Rows 9–16). Work St st on the sole.

After 2 pattern repeats of the Tulip Pattern are completed, continue in St st all around until sock is 2 in./5 cm from desired finished length.

Adding beads to the cuff

Working the heel in back-and-forth rows

Turning the heel, right end

Turning the heel, left end

Picking up selvedge stitches

Decreasing for the toe

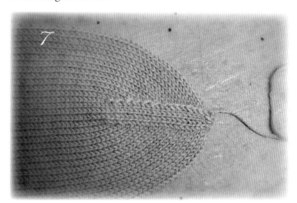

The completed paired-decrease toe section

Paired-Decrease Toe

Transfer the 32 upper foot sts to needles 1 and 2, the 32 sole sts to needles 3 and 4.

Decrease: Across instep sts on needles 1 and 2, k1, skp, knit to last 3 sts on needle 2, k2tog, k1; repeat across the sole sts on needles 3 and 4—4 sts dec.

Repeat these decreases in every other row, 6 times in all.

Now, decrease in every row until 8 sts are left.

Pull the yarn tail through the remaining 8 sts to close the gap.

Weave in all tails.

Sew on woven ribbon at the outside of the leg over the column of 6 knit sts.

Work the left sock mirror-inverted.

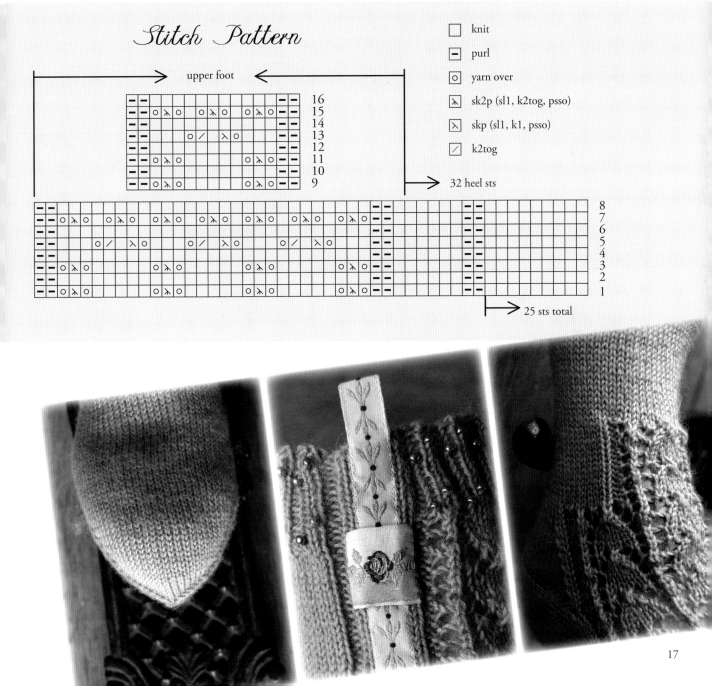

Stitch Pattern

upper foot

32 heel sts

25 sts total

knit	□
purl	−
yarn over	o
sk2p (sl1, k2tog, psso)	⅄
skp (sl1, k1, psso)	\
k2tog	/

Debutante Arm Warmers

An accessory to fall in love with: Arm warmers with delicate lace edging.

Finished Measurements

9 in./23 cm long

Yarn

Pearl cotton #8 (shown in DMC Petra Art. 993; 100% cotton, twice mercerized; 306 yd./280 m per 3.5 oz./100g skein; Pebble Grey and Red)

- 306 yd./280 m gray
- 306 yd./280 m medium red

Needles and Other Materials

- US 0 (2 mm) set of 5 double-pointed needles
- US 7 (1.5 mm) steel crochet hook
- Smoke gray and pink seed beads
- 6 slightly larger pink/beige pearl beads
- 4 in./10 cm woven jacquard ribbon with red flowers
- 14 in./35 cm woven jacquard ribbon with leafy vine pattern
- Tapestry needle
- Sewing needle and thread
- Basting pins (optional)
- Steam iron

Gauge

41 sts in [k2, p2] rib = 4 in./10 cm

Sleeve

With dark gray, cast on 75 sts, join into round, and distribute evenly over 4 DPNs.

Work the charted pattern on page 21 for 6 in./15 cm, repeating Rows 1–4. In the *last* repeat of Row 4 only, increase 1 st for a total of 76 sts.

Work [k2, p2] ribbing for 1.5 in./4 cm, then bind off all sts loosely.

Lace

Crochet lace as shown on chart below directly onto bound off sts.

Finishing

Weave in all tails.

Carefully sew woven jacquard ribbon into stockinette center of arm warmer, slightly stretching knitted fabric to prevent puckering of ribbon when worn. At edge of arm warmer, fold leafy vine ribbon into .75 in./1.5 cm loop and sew on. Sew on a piece of the red rose ribbon at the wrist, as shown.

String and sew beads along the edge of the flower ribbon, as shown. Carefully steam iron crocheted edging.

Crochet Chart

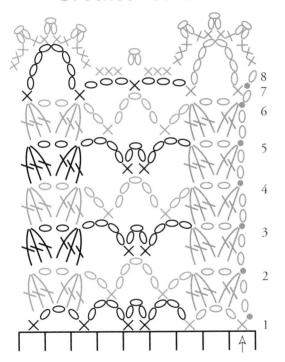

◯	chain
✕	single crochet
⋀	dc3tog
⬭	picot [ch3, sc into the first ch]
↑	begin
●	slip stitch
⎍	knit stitch

Stitch Pattern

☐	knit
⊟	purl
◯	yarn over
⋀	p2tog

5 x

Delicate Lace

One can never have too many decorative
and passionate pieces like these, created
with lots of love and fine thread.

Gossamer Shawl

This unusual wrap of gossamer-thin knitted lace is a real beauty.

Yarn

Lace weight #0 mohair/silk yarn (shown in Permin Angel; 70% kid mohair, 30% silk; 230 yd./210 m per 0.9 oz./25 g skein; Pebble Grey)
- 460 yd./420 m gray

Pearl cotton #8 (shown in DMC Petra Art. 993; 100% cotton, twice mercerized; 306 yd./280 m per 3.5 oz./100g skein; Pebble Grey)
- 306 yd./280 m gray

Pearl crochet thread
- Small amounts of forest green, ecru, and light drab brown

Needles and Other Materials
- US 8 (5 mm) circular knitting needles (varying lengths, increase length as needed to accommodate stitches)
- US 4 (3.5 mm) circular knitting needle, 32 in./81 cm long
- US B-1 (2.25 mm) or C-2 (2.75 mm) crochet hook
- Tapestry needle
- 2 pieces of cotton fabric, cream and tan striped, each measuring 5 x 1.5 in./13 x 3.5 cm
- 4 in./10 cm woven jacquard ribbon with rose bud print

Gauge

16 sts in St st with lace weight yarn and US 8 (5 mm) needles = 4 in./10 cm

Notes
- This shawl is worked top-down, starting at the nape.

Shawl

With lace weight yarn and US 8 (5 mm) circular needle, cast on 5 sts. Purl one row.

Continue from chart. In even-numbered rows, purl all sts. The first and last st are selvedge sts. In every odd-numbered row, you will increase by 4 sts, as shown on the chart. Continue working in established pattern until there are 140 knit sts on either side of the center st (not counting the yo's on both sides of the ctr st) until there are 285 sts on the needles.

Change to gray pearl cotton thread and US 4 (3.5 mm) needle.

Next row: Work [k1, yo] into each st to the end of the row, doubling the st count.

Purl all sts in WS row.

Next row: Work [k1, yo] into each st to the end of the row, doubling the st count once more.

Purl all sts in WS row.

Continue in established pattern: 1 selvedge st, k12, yo, k to ctr st, yo, k1, yo, k to the last 13 sts, yo, k12, k the selv st. Purl all sts in WS row. Work 9 more rows in established pattern.

Next RS row: Using crochet hook, grasp 4 sts together and crochet them off together as a slip stitch, followed by a chain of 6. Repeat [sl st 4 tog, ch6] until all sts are bound off.

Weave in all ends and carefully steam iron shawl.

Decorative Flowers

Following the instructions on page 61, use pearl crochet thread and crochet six one-row three-dimensional blossoms.

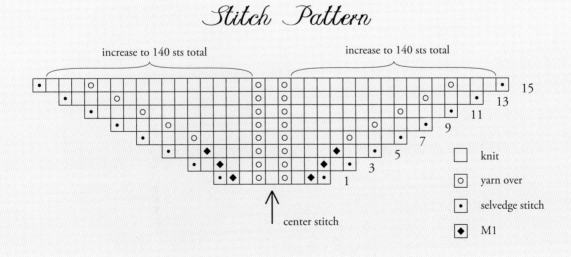

Stitch Pattern

increase to 140 sts total   increase to 140 sts total

15
13
11
9
7
5
3
1

center stitch

☐ knit
☐ yarn over (with o)
☐ selvedge stitch (with •)
◆ M1

Crochet four stems, two consisting of 100 chain sts each and two
    others 30 chains long.

Knot a blossom onto the longer stem, thread the free end through the
    selvedge st at the end of the lace yarn, and knot another blossom to
    the end of the stem. Knot a blossom onto one of the shorter stems
    and thread the free end through the selvedge st.

Wrap the stem with a strip of cotton fabric (as explained on page 62),
    adding woven jacquard ribbon into the roll towards the end, and
    sew the completed roll onto the stem.

Make an identical second blossom arrangement and attach it to the
    other edge of the shawl.

Mohair Arm Warmers

These elegant arm warmers will
make you feel like a queen.

Finished Measurements

18.5 in./47 cm long

Yarn

Lace weight #0 mohair/silk yarn (shown in Permin Angel; 70% kid mohair, 30% silk; 230 yd./210 m per 0.9 oz./25 g skein; Pebble Grey)

• 230 yd./210 m gray

Pearl cotton #8 (shown in DMC Petra Art. 993; 100% cotton, twice mercerized; 306 yd./280 m per 3.5 oz./100g skein; Pebble Grey)

• 306 yd./280 m gray

Pearl crochet thread

• Small amounts of forest green, ecru, and light drab brown

Needles and Other Materials

• US 8 (5 mm) set of 5 double-pointed needles
• US 6 (4 mm) set of 5 double-pointed needles
• US 4 (3.5 mm) set of 5 double-pointed needles
• US B-1 (2.25 mm) or C-2 (2.75 mm) crochet hook
• Stretchy brown velvet ribbon (twice as long as wrist circumference)
• 4 in./10 cm woven jacquard ribbon with rose bud pattern
• Tapestry needle
• Sewing needle and matching thread

Gauge

16 sts in St st with lace weight yarn and US 8 (5mm) needles = 4 in./10 cm

Arm Warmer

With lace weight yarn and US 8 (5 mm) DPNs, cast on 36 sts, join into round and divide evenly onto 4 DPNs.

Work in [k2, p2] ribbing for 1.5 in./4 cm.

Now, work in St st for 14 in./35 cm.

Change to US 6 (4 mm) DPNs and work [k2, p2] ribbing for 2.5 in./6 cm.

Work an **eyelet row**: [Yo, k2tog] to end of round.

Work in St st for 1.2 in./3 cm.

Change to light gray #8 pearl cotton thread and US 4 (3.5 mm) DPNs. Now, double the stitch count by working [k1, yo] into every stitch.

Next row: Knit all sts.

Double the stitch count once more by working [k1, yo] into every stitch.

Work in St st for 9 rounds.

Finishing

For the crocheted edge, grasp 4 sts at once with a crochet hook and sc4tog, then chain 6. [Sc4tog, ch6] to end of round.

Weave in all ends.

Thread a piece of stretchy velvet, twice as long as your wrist circumference, through the eyelet row and seam the ends together.

Using pearl crochet thread and crochet hook, make three one-row three-dimensional crocheted flowers (see page 61) with chain-stitch stems in three different lengths: 1 in., 2 in., and 3 in.

Position the woven jacquard ribbon, folded double, over the seam of the velvet ribbon and attach the flower arrangement to it, hiding the ends of the stems.

Lacy Knit Skirt

Wear your hand-knit creation for a night on the town.

Finished Measurements

Sizes 2/4 (6/8, 10/12)

Yarn

Lace weight #1 mohair/silk yarn (shown in Permin Angel; 70% kid mohair, 30% silk; 230 yd./210 m per 0.9 oz./25 g skein; Pebble Grey)

• 460 yd./420 m gray
• 230 yd./210 m white

Pearl cotton #8 (shown in DMC Petra Art. 993; 100% cotton, twice mercerized; 306 yd./280 m per 3.5 oz./100g skein; Pebble Grey)

• 306 yd./280 m gray

Needles and Other Materials

• US 8 (5 mm) circular knitting needle, 24 in./60 cm long
• US 4 (3.5 mm) circular knitting needle, 24 in./60 cm long
• US B-1 (2.25 mm) or C-2 (2.75 mm) crochet hook
• Black elastic, 1.5 in./4 cm wide, sized for the waistband
• Tapestry needle
• Sewing needle and matching thread for seaming elastic

Gauge

16 sts in St st with lace weight yarn and US 8 (5 mm) needles = 4 in./10 cm

Gray Layer

With gray lace weight yarn and US 8 (5 mm) circular needle, cast on 132 (140, 148) sts and join into round.

Work [k2, p2] ribbing in the round for 4 in./10 cm.

Increase round: Work in St st, increasing 0 (1, 2) sts for a total of 132 (141, 150) sts.

Continue in St st for 14 in./36 cm.

Eyelet round: *K1, k2tog, yo. Rep from * to end of round.

Next 5 rounds: Work in St st.

Change to US 4 (3.5 mm) needle and light gray #8 pearl cotton thread. Double your stitch count by working [k1, yo] into every stitch of the round.

Next round: Knit all sts.

Next round: Double your stitch count once more by working [k1, yo] into every stitch.

Work in St st for 9 rounds.

Crocheted edging: Using crochet hook, grasp 4 sts and sc them together, followed by a chain of 6. Continue with [sc4tog, ch6] until all sts are bound off.

White Layer

Turn skirt inside out, WS facing. Using crochet hook (and placing on US 8 needle) and white lace weight yarn, pick up all 132 (141, 150) sts from the next-to-last gray lace yarn round.

Work 5 rounds in St st, increasing 12 (11, 10) stitches evenly spaced in first round for a total of 144 (152, 160) sts.

Continue from chart, repeating Rounds 1 and 2 nine times in all to complete Rounds 1–18, then working rounds 19 to 24 once.

Bind off all sts with a crochet hook as explained in the Delicate Shoulder Wrap pattern on page 13.

Fold half of the waistband to the inside and sew it on by hand not too tightly, leaving a small opening for inserting the elastic.

Insert elastic into waistband and sew both ends of the elastic together.

Weave in all ends.

Gently steam iron the skirt.

Stitch Pattern

	24
	23
	22
	21
	20
	19
	2
	1

□ knit

− purl

○ yarn over

⅄ sk2p (sl1, k2tog, psso)

⅄ skp (sl1, k1, psso)

∕ k2tog

ℓ k1-tbl

Spa Slippers

Whimsical details adorn these enchanting slippers. Ribbons, beads and crocheted flowers turn them into truly unique pieces.

Finished Measurements

Sizes US 6.5–7.5 (8–9, 9.5–10)

Yarn

For gray slippers: Super fine weight #1 sock yarn (shown in Permin BabySock; 80% wool, 20% polyamide; 230 yd./210 m per 1.8 oz./50 g skein; Grey)

- 230 yd./210 m gray

Lace weight #0 mohair/silk yarn (shown in Permin Angel; 70% kid mohair, 30% silk; 230 yd./210 m per 0.9 oz./25 g skein; Crème)

- 230 yd./210 m off-white

For lavender slippers: Super fine weight #1 sock yarn (shown in Permin BabySock; 80% wool, 20% polyamide; 230 yd./210 m per 1.8 oz./50 g skein; Lavender)

- 230 yd./210 m lavender

Lace weight #0 mohair/silk yarn (shown in Permin Angel; 70% kid mohair, 30% silk; 230 yd./210 m per 0.9 oz./25 g skein; Purple)

- 230 yd./210 m purple

Needles and Other Materials

- US 8 (5 mm) straight knitting needles
- US B-1 (2.25 mm) crochet hook
- Silver-gold mini beads
- Sewing needle and thread
- Tapestry needle
- For lavender slippers only: 16 in./40 cm lavender grosgrain ribbon
- Steam iron or garment steamer

Gauge

22 sts in St st in super fine weight sock yarn with yarn held double = 4 in./10 cm

Slipper (Make 2)

Basic pattern is for both models. Work with yarn held double throughout.

Cast on 59 (63, 67) sts.

Work the sole in garter stitch, as follows.

Row 1 (WS): Knit all sts and mark the center stitch.

Row 2 (Increase): M1, k1, M1, k to ctr st, M1, k1, M1, k to last st, M1, k1, M1—6 sts increased.

Repeat Increase Row every other row 4 more times until you have 89 (93, 97) sts in Row 10.

For the sides, in Rows 11–15, work in St st, marking the middle 7 sts.

Row 16 (Decrease Row): K1, [p2, k2] 5 times, k to 3 sts before first marker, k3tog, sm, k to m, sm, k3tog-tbl, k17 (19, 21), [k2, p2] 5 times, k1.

Row 17: Work even in pattern (knit the knits, purl the purls; no increases or decreases).

Row 18: Work Decrease as Row 16, decreasing 2 sts before the first m and 2 sts after the second marker and working rib pattern as established.

Row 19: Work even in pattern.

Continue repeating decreases in every other row until there are 49 (49, 49) sts left.

Purl 1 row.

Bind off all sts tightly.

Seam the sole and heel and weave in all ends.

Make a second slipper the same way.

Finishing

Gray Slippers

Pre-thread 20 beads (for each slipper) onto mohair yarn.

Round 1: Sc2 into every bound-off stitch.

Round 2: [Sc1, ch6] into every fifth st.

Round 3: Sl st 3 to middle st of first chain arc, then [sc1, ch6] into middle st of every subsequent chain arc.

Round 4: Sl st 3 to middle st of first chain arc, then [sc1, ch3, ch1 with bead, ch3] into middle st of every subsequent chain arc.

Weave in ends and gently steam block lace.

Lavender Slippers

Work a shell edging into the bound off sts, as follows: [Sc1, dc5, sc1] into every other stitch. Repeat to end of round.

Make two three-dimensional crocheted flowers as explained on page 61, with stems 4 in./10 cm long each.

Using 8 in./20 cm grosgrain ribbon for each one, make two bows and attach them to the slippers.

Decorate the flowers with beads and sew them onto the bows.

Weave in all ends.

Flower–Adorned Hat

Turn out in style with this chic hat.

Finished Measurements

Circumference: 13 in./33 cm at ribbed brim (unstretched)

Yarn

Lace weight #0 mohair/silk yarn (shown in Permin Angel; 70% kid mohair, 30% silk; 230 yd./210 m per 0.9 oz./25 g skein; Purple)
- 230 yd./210 m purple

Super fine weight #1 sock yarn (shown in Permin BabySock; 80% wool, 20% polyamide; 230 yd./210 m per 1.8 oz./50 g skein; Lavender and Grey-Tan)
- 230 yd./210 m lavender
- 230 yd./210 m grayish tan

Needles and Other Materials

- US 8 (5 mm) set of 5 double-pointed needles
- US 1.5 (2.5 mm) set of 5 double-pointed needles
- US B-1 (2.25 mm) crochet hook
- 3 cream pearl beads
- Small purple beads
- 4 in./10 cm woven jacquard ribbon with flower and vine design
- Tapestry needle
- Sewing needle and matching thread

Gauge

16 sts in St st with lace weight yarn and US 8 (5 mm) needles = 4 in./10 cm

48 sts in [k2, p2] rib with super fine weight yarn and US 1.5 (2.5 mm) needles = 4 in./10 cm

Hat

This hat is worked top-down in stockinette stitch in the round (knit all rounds).

With US 8 (5 mm) DPNs and lace weight yarn, cast on 4 sts, join to work in the round, and distribute evenly onto 4 DPNs.

Round 1: Work in St st—4 sts.

Round 2: [K1, M1] 4 times—8 sts. (M1 is explained on page 56.)

All following odd rounds: Knit all sts.

All following even rounds: [K to last st on each needle, M1] 4 times.

Repeat last two rounds until there are 160 sts on the needles.

Change to US 1.5 (2.5 mm) DPNs and super fine yarn and work in [k2, p2] ribbing for 12 rounds.

Next round (eyelet round): [K2tog, yo] to end of round.

Work 12 more rounds of [k2, p2] ribbing and bind off all sts.

Finishing

Using the eyelet round as a fold line, fold half of ribbed section inward and sew on loosely by hand.

Weave in all ends.

Using grayish tan and lavender yarn, make one two-row and two one-row three-dimensional crocheted flowers (see instructions on page 61).

Decorate flowers with beads and attach flower arrangement above brim at side of hat. Fold woven ribbon in half with ends folded under and sew to cuff of hat next to flowers.

Romantic Loop

Dress it up, dress it down. This infinity loop goes with every outfit.

Finished Measurements

Circumference: 51 in./130 cm

Width: 12 in./30.5 cm

Yarn

Lace weight #0 mohair/silk yarn (shown in Permin Angel; 70% kid mohair, 30% silk; 230 yd./210 m per 0.9 oz./25 g skein; Lavender)

• 460 yd./420 m lavender

Pearl cotton #8 (shown in DMC Petra Art. 993; 100% cotton, twice mercerized; 306 yd./280 m per 3.5 oz./100g skein; Light Grey)

• 306 yd./280 m light gray

Needles and Other Materials

• US 7 (4.5 mm) straight or circular knitting needles (to accommodate 70 sts)
• US 1.5 (2.5 mm) straight or circular knitting needles
• 10 in./25 cm woven jacquard ribbon in heart and vine pattern
• 10 in./25 cm woven jacquard ribbon in berry vine pattern
• Tapestry needle
• Sewing needle and matching thread

Gauge

23 sts in [k2, p2] rib with lace weight yarn and US 7 (4.5 mm) needles = 4 in./10 cm (gauge is not critical for this project)

Scarf

This loop is worked flat. For selvedge sts, ktbl first st of row, slip last st of row.

Using US 7 (4.5 mm) needles and lace weight yarn, cast on 70 sts.

Row 1 (RS): K1-tbl, [k2, p2] to last st, sl1.

Row 2 (WS): K1-tbl, [p2, k2] to last st, sl1.

Repeat Rows 1–2 until piece is 47 in./120 cm long.

Change to cotton thread and US 1.5 (2.5 mm) needles.

Row 1 (RS): K1-tbl, k to last st, sl1.

Row 2 (WS): K1-tbl, k3, p62, k3, sl1.

Repeat Rows 1–2 four times more for a total of 10 rows worked.

Row 11 (RS): K1-tbl, k3, p62, k3, sl1.

Row 12 (WS): K1-tbl, k to last st, sl1.

Row 13 (RS): Repeat Row 11.

Row 14 (WS): Repeat Row 11.

Rows 15–34: Repeat Rows 1–2 ten times more.

Finishing

Bind off all sts.

Sew woven ribbons onto gray section of scarf by hand.

Sew beginning and end of scarf together to form a loop.

Azure Arm Warmers

A bit of romance for a chilly evening.

Finished Measurement

Length: 9 in./23 cm

Yarn

Pearl cotton #8 (shown in DMC Petra Art. 993; 100% cotton, twice mercerized; 306 yd./280 m per 3.5 oz./100 g skein; Grey)

- 306 yd./280 m gray

Lace weight #0 mohair/silk yarn (shown in Permin Angel; 70% kid mohair, 30% silk; 230 yd./210 m per 0.9 oz./25 g skein; Blue)

- 230 yd./210 m blue

Needles and Other Materials

- US 0 (2 mm) set of 5 double-pointed needles
- US 6 (4 mm) set of 5 double-pointed needles
- US 7 (1.5 mm) crochet hook
- 4 in./10 cm woven jacquard ribbon with rose vine pattern
- 10 in./25 cm woven jacquard ribbon in leafy vine pattern
- Tiny silver-gold beads
- Tapestry needle
- Sewing needle and matching thread
- Steam iron

Gauge

41 sts in [k2, p2] rib with pearl cotton and US 0 (2 mm) needles = 4 in./10 cm

Arm Warmer

With US 0 (2 mm) DPNs and crochet cotton, cast on 68 sts, join to work in the round, and distribute evenly onto 4 DPNs.

Work in [k2, p2] ribbing for 1.2 in./3 cm.

Now, work in charted stitch pattern for 5 in./13 cm.

Change to US 6 (4 mm) DPNs and lace weight yarn.

Next round: [K1, yo] into every stitch of the round—136 sts.

Work in St st for 13 rounds.

Crocheted Edging

Thread 34 beads onto crochet cotton thread. Follow steps 1–4 below; see page 42 for step-by-step photos.

Step 1: With crochet hook, grasp 4 live sts from your knitting.

Step 2: Pull the working yarn through all 4 sts together, then ch4.

Step 3: Work a picot as follows: Ch2, ch1 with bead, sc into first of all three chains.

Step 4: Ch4 again.

Repeat Steps 1–4 until all sts are crocheted off, remembering that the third chain in the picot is always a beaded one.

Finishing

Weave in all ends.

Carefully sew woven jacquard ribbon to stockinette section of arm warmers, as shown, slightly stretching knitted fabric to prevent puckering of ribbon when worn.

Gently steam ruffled edge.

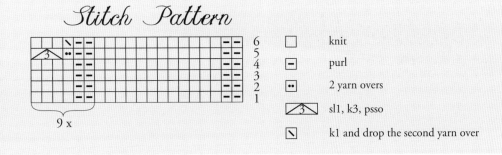

Stitch Pattern

	knit
−	purl
••	2 yarn overs
/3\	sl1, k3, psso
﹨	k1 and drop the second yarn over

9 x

Crocheted edging with incorporated beads.

Treasure Pouch Poncho

There's lots of space to snuggle up in this cozy poncho! The strap with pocket detail makes this piece unique.

Measurements

Front and back measure 27 in./68.5 cm across. One size fits most. To adjust size, use slightly smaller or larger needles and lighter or heavier yarn and adjust your gauge in bobble pattern to reach your desired width (95 sts across).

Yarn

Bulky weight #5 wool/linen yarn (shown in Permin Carmen; 85% wool, 15% linen; 55 yd./50 m per 1.8 oz./50 g skein; Grey)
• 990 yd./900 m gray

Needles and Other Materials

• US 15 (10 mm) 24 in./60 cm circular needle
• US 15 (10 mm) set of 5 double-pointed needles
• Stitch holder (able to accommodate chunky yarn) or thick piece of waste yarn
• Tapestry needle

Gauge

14 sts in bobble pattern = 4 in./10 cm.

Special Stitch

M1p-tbl: Pick up the bar between the stitches on the needles from front to back with the left-hand needle and purl it through the back loop.

Notes

• The back and front are worked flat and seamed at the sides and shoulders, with a cowl neck added at the end.
• The bobble stitch pattern will appear on the wrong side of the fabric as you work the stitch, i.e., start Row 1 of pattern on WS of poncho to have bobbles appear on the outside when worn.

Back

Cast on 76 sts with US 15 (10 mm) circular needle.
Work 7 rows in [k2, p2] ribbing.

Row 8: Knit all sts, evenly distributing 19 increases—95 sts.
Work charted stitch pattern for 17 in./43 cm. Odd rows are read from right to left, even rows from left to right.
In the next RS row, to make the slit for the strap, bind off the middle 5 of the 7 knit sts in the pattern repeat and cast on 5 new sts in the same spot in the following WS row, using backward loop cast-on or your preferred method, as follows:

Slit Row 1 (RS): Work pattern repeat to just having finished the "13x repeat," k1, BO 5, k1, continue from chart to end of row.

Slit Row 2 (WS): Work pattern repeat to just having finished the "7x repeat," p1, CO 5, p1, continue from chart to end of row.

Work 4 regular rows in charted pattern (without forming a slit).

Slit Row 7 (RS): Repeat Slit Row 1.

Slit Row 8 (WS): Repeat Slit Row 2.

One set of two slits has been created.
Continue in charted pattern until piece is 23 in./58 cm long.
Work Slit Rows 1–8 once more to create a second set of slits.
Continue working in charted pattern until piece is 26 in./66 cm long.

Back Neckline Shaping

Transfer 8 center sts to a stitch holder or piece of waste yarn. From here on, left and right back are worked separately, continuing to work in established pattern. You can leave the right back sts on the needle while working on the left back, or you may want to put them aside on a spare circular.

Stitch Pattern

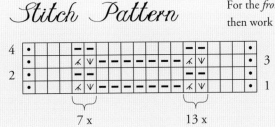

For the *front*, work 7 repeats width-wise where it says 13 (before the St st column), then work 13 repeats where it says 7 (after the St st column).

•	selvedge stitch
☐	knit
–	purl
⅄	p3tog
V	[k1, yo, k1] into the same st

Left back neckline shaping: In next RS row, bind off 2 sts
at beginning of row (at the side of the neck opening).
Continue to work in pattern until 16 sts are left. Bind off
these sts.

Right back neckline shaping: In following WS row, bind off 2
sts at beginning of row (at the side of the neck opening).
Continue to work in pattern until 16 sts are left. Bind off
these sts.

Front

*For the front, to place the St st column with the slits for the strap on
the right half of the front, work 7 repeats of the 2-stitch-column
marked "13x" in the chart, work the St st column, then work 13
repeats of the 2-stitch-column marked "7x." You do not have to
reverse the charts, only exchange "7x" and "13x."*

*The front is worked the same as the back, with the exception that the
strap slits are on the right half of the front, and neckline shaping
starts earlier, when piece is 24.5 in./62 cm long.*

Cast on 76 sts with circular needle.

Work 7 rows in [k2, p2] ribbing.

Row 8: Knit all sts, evenly distributing 19 increases—95 sts.

Work charted stitch pattern for 17 in./43 cm. Odd rows are read
from right to left, even rows from left to right. As explained in the
note above, for the front only, first work 7 repeats of the two-
stitch column marked "13x" width-wise, continue from chart,
then repeat 13 repeats width-wise of the other two-stitch column
marked "7x."

For the slit, in the next RS row, you will bind off the middle 5 of the
7 knit sts in the pattern repeat and cast on 5 new sts in the same
spot in the following WS row.

Slit Row 1 (RS): Work pattern repeat to just having finished the "13x
repeat" (remember, for the front, you repeated it only 7 times
width-wise), k1, BO 5, k1, continue from chart to end of row (13
times width-wise where it says "7x").

Slit Row 2 (WS): Work pattern repeat to just having finished the "7x
repeat" (remember, you repeated it 13 times here),
p1, CO 5, p1, continue from chart to end of row (7 times width-
wise where it says "13x").

Work 4 regular rows in charted pattern (without forming a slit).

Slit Row 7 (RS): Repeat Slit Row 1.

Slit Row 8 (WS): Repeat Slit Row 2.

One set of two slits has been created.

Continue in charted pattern until piece is 23 in./58 cm long.

Work Slit Rows 1–8 once more to create a second set of slits.

Continue working in charted pattern until piece is 24.5 in./62 cm
long.

Front Neckline Shaping

Transfer 8 center sts to a stitch holder or piece of waste yarn. From
here on, left and right front are worked separately, continuing to
work in established pattern. You can leave the right front sts on
the needle while working on the left front, or you may want to put
them aside on a spare circular.

Left front neckline shaping: In next RS row, bind off 2 sts at beginning
of row (at the side of the neck opening). Continue to work in
pattern until 16 sts are left. Bind off these sts.

Right front neckline shaping: In following WS row, bind off 2 sts at
beginning of row (at the side of the neck opening). Continue to
work in pattern until 16 sts are left. Bind off these sts.

Cowl Neck Collar

In inclement weather, this cowl collar can double as a hood.

With right sides facing, place front piece onto back piece and close the
shoulder seams.

Starting at the left shoulder on the front, pick up and knit 16 sts from
the left edge of the neck opening, then transfer the 8 center front
sts to your working needle, pick up and knit 16 sts from the right
edge of the neck opening, transfer the 8 center back sts to your
working needle—48 sts for the collar.

Work in [k2, p1] ribbing for 10 rounds.

Increase Round: [K2, p1, M1p-tbl] to end of round—64 sts.

Work in [k2, p2] ribbing for 18 rounds—64 sts.

Increase Round: [K1, p1, M1p-tbl, p1] 16 times—80 sts.

Work in [k2, p3] ribbing for 24 rounds—80 sts.

Next round: Knit.

Next round: Work Round 2 in Bobble pattern from chart.

Next round: Knit.

Next round: Work Round 3 in Bobble pattern from chart.

Next round: Knit.

Next round: Bind off all sts.

Seaming Sides

From the RS and starting at the bottom of the poncho, close side
seams in mattress stitch, leaving the last 9 in./22 cm at the top
open for armholes.

Weave in all ends.

Velvet Band and Pouch
Materials Needed

- Pearl crochet thread in pearl gray, pewter gray, and very light
  antique blue
- US 7 (1.5 mm) steel crochet hook
- Hand sewing needle
- Large tapestry needle
- Small snap closure for closing pouch
- Large snap closure for attaching pouch band to poncho
- Smoke gray mini beads
- Polyester filling
- 83 in./210 cm light gray velvet ribbon, cut into 2 pieces, 43.5
  in./110 cm and 39.5 in./100 cm
- 43.5 in./110 cm woven jacquard ribbon in blue leafy vine pattern
- 12 in./30 cm gray-blue grosgrain ribbon
- 12 in./30 cm gray-blue bobbin lace
- 8 in./20 cm tan linen fabric
- Embroidery floss in dark blue, turquoise, medium blue, and green
- 14 x 12 in./35 x 30 cm solid pastel blue cotton fabric
- 4 in./10 cm cotton fabric for the heart
- Sewing machine
- Embroidery pattern on page 48
- Pouch and Heart patterns on page 49

Fold the piece of blue cotton fabric to a size of 12 x 7 in./30 x 17.5 cm.

Make two transfers of the Pouch pattern, placing the straight edge
of template (top of pouch) onto fabric fold. Add sufficient seam
allowance, about .5 in./1.25 cm on each side. One of the two will
form the outside of the pouch, the other the lining. Cut out both
pieces and unfold each one of them separately. Right sides facing,
place them on top of each other, and, starting before the rounded
corner at a narrow side, seam around, leaving a small opening
for turning out after turning the last corner, on the narrow side
where you started (this will be the bottom of the lining). The
other narrow side (bottom of the outside) has been seamed. At the
round corners, make small evenly spaced incisions into the seam
allowances to prevent puckering. Serge or zigzag around the seam
allowance for extra protection.

Turn seamed piece inside out by pressing the seamed narrow side into
the tube with a ruler. The tube is now turned, the seams are hidden
inside, but the tube is still long. Seam the turning opening (inside
bottom) by hand and, grasping the fabric with both thumbs in the
middle of the tube, at the fabric fold from cutting, move lining
down inside bag until fabric fold from cutting is the top of bag and
the bottoms meet.

Sew grosgrain ribbon (begin and end meeting at the front) and bobbin
lace to the top edge of the pouch, forming a small loop of satin
ribbon at the back of the pouch.

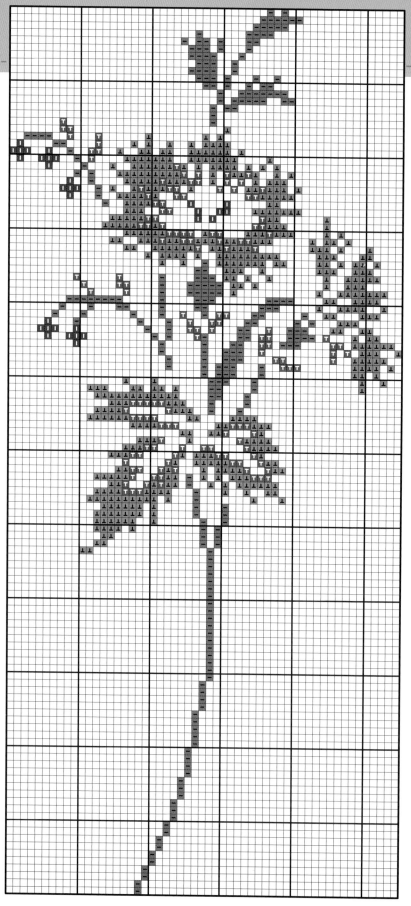

Attach a snap closure at the center of the inside of the top edge of the pouch.

Using crochet hook and pearl crochet thread, crochet three large "Crocheted Beads" as described on page 49.

Using crochet hook and pearl crochet thread in a contrasting color, crochet a 14 in./35 cm long chain and slip stitch back over the chains.

Sew crocheted bead onto one end of crocheted chain. Draw crocheted chain through turned under end of grosgrain ribbon, then sew a second crocheted bead to the other end of the chain to secure in place.

Sew woven jacquard ribbon along center of long velvet ribbon, folding jacquard ribbon ends under by 2 in./5 cm. Fold cut edges of velvet ribbon under by 1 in./2.5 cm and sew on at fold line, leaving the sides open for threading crocheted chains later. Attach the little pouch at one end as shown.

Sew the embroidered piece flush onto the velvet ribbon, folding seam allowance under, at 10 in./25 cm upward from the end with the pouch.

Decorate embroidery with beads.

Using Heart pattern, cut out and sew a small heart.

Crochet a chain 9 in./22 cm long, reinforcing it by slip stitching back over the chains, and sew the heart onto this chain.

Thread crocheted chain through free end of velvet ribbon and sew third crocheted bead to end of chain. Knot the crocheted chain.

Embroidery Chart

▦	dark blue
⊥⊥	turquoise
⊤⊤	medium blue
▬▬	green

Thread the completed pouch band through the slits in the poncho and secure it on the shoulder with the large snap closure. The part with the stud goes onto the RS of the knitting, the socket part on the underside of the velvet band.

Crocheted Bead (Small or Large)

Materials

- Pearl crochet thread
- US 7 (1.5 mm) steel crochet hook
- Sewing needle
- Polyester filling

Ch2. Sc6 into the first chain. Sl st to join to a round.

Continue in spiral rounds with shifting beginning of round, starting from these 6 sts.

Increase: Sc2 into each sc of the previous round, until you have 16 sts (8 times).

Now, [sc2in1, sc1] around until you have 22 sts for a small bead or 24 sts for a large bead.

Working even: Once you have reached the stitch count for your size, sc around for 6 to 7 rounds. No increases.

Decrease: For both sizes, [sc2, sk1] until you have 16 sts in the round again.

Continue decreasing, both sizes: [sc1, sk1] until 4 sts are left.

Stuff the bead tightly with polyester fill. With sewing needle, thread the yarn through the last loop and close the gap.

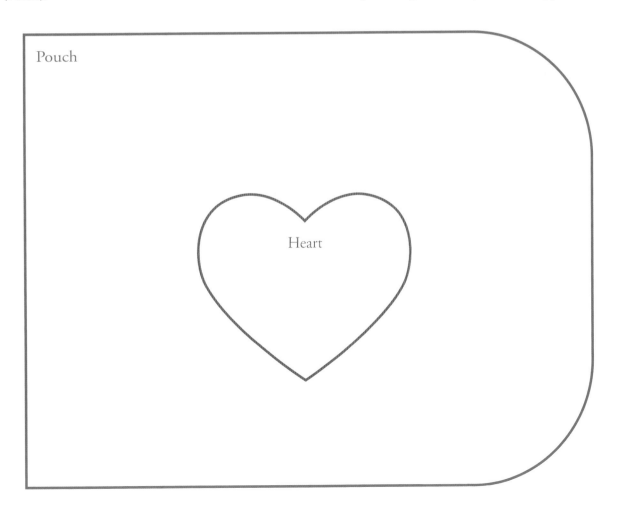

Pouch

Heart

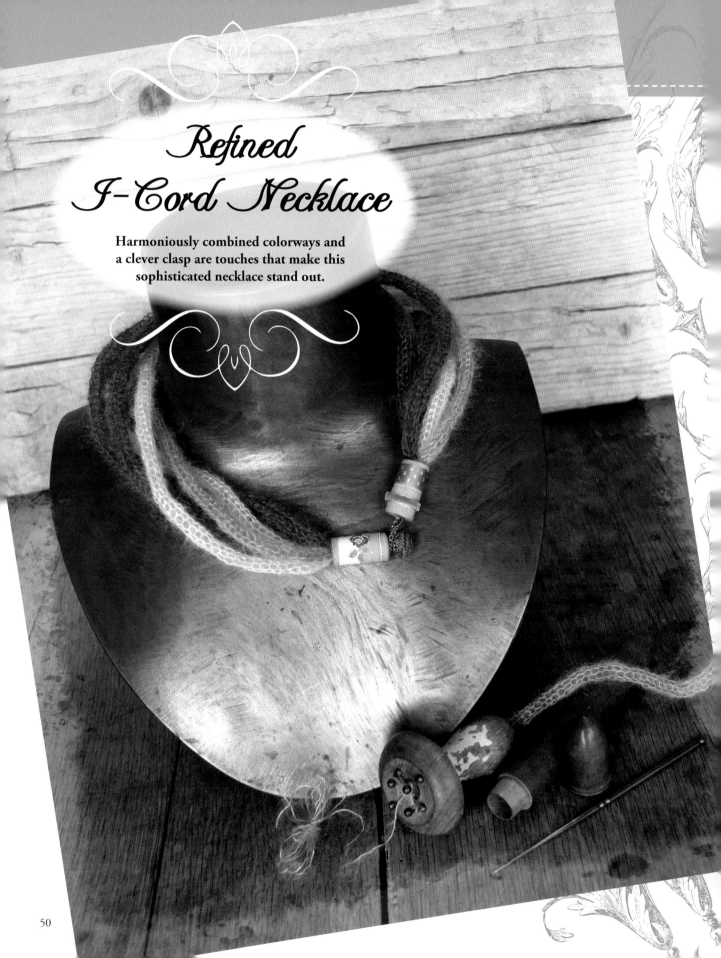

Refined
I-Cord Necklace

Harmoniously combined colorways and
a clever clasp are touches that make this
sophisticated necklace stand out.

Measurements

Length: 24 in./60 cm

Yarn

Lace weight #0 mohair/silk yarn (shown in Permin Angel; 70% kid mohair, 30% silk; 230 yd./210 m per 0.9 oz./25 g skein; Cream, Tan, and Pebble Grey)

- 230 yd./210 m off-white
- 230 yd./210 m tan
- 230 yd./210 m gray

Pearl crochet thread

- Small amount of dark beige gray

Needles and Other Materials

- US 7 (1.5 mm) steel crochet hook
- 2 strips of solid natural-colored cotton fabric, each 7 x 2 in./18 x 5 cm
- 2 in./5 cm woven jacquard ribbon in antique rose vine pattern
- 2 in./5 cm satin ribbon in pastel blue and tan

- 2 in./5 cm velvet ribbon in gray brown
- I-cord tool (spool loom) with 4 pegs (or 2 double-pointed needles)

Necklace

Make 6 I-cords (2 cream, 1 tan, 3 gray), each between 21.5 in./54 cm and 25 in./64 cm long.

Crochet a small bead as follows:

Ch2. Sc6 into the first chain. Join to a round.

Continue in spiral rounds with shifting beginning of round, starting from these 6 sts.

Increase: [Sc2] into each sc of the previous round, until you have 20 sts (10 times).

Sc for one round.

Decrease: [Sc1, sk1] until 4 sts are left.

Ch10, work 1 sl st into each chain.

For the loop: Ch30. Starting to work into the tenth chain, work 1 sl st into each chain until you are back at the beginning of the chain.

From one of the cotton strips, make a drum roll as shown on page 62, making sure to secure with stitches the beginning chains of the loop and those of the I-cords within. Continue winding the roll as instructed, adding in the ribbon toward the end.

Create another roll from the remaining cotton strip, securing the crocheted bead and the ends of the I-cords with a few stitches as well.

Making I-cord with a Spool Loom

Insert the beginning tail of the yarn through the opening in the I-cord tool until it exits the bottom opening.

Thread the yarn around the four pegs of the spool by leading it around the first peg counterclockwise, then moving to the next peg in clockwise direction (illustration 1) until all four pegs are covered.

To form the first loop, lead the yarn in the front from right to left over the first peg, above the layer of yarn from the first round. With crochet hook or tool that came with the loom, grab the loop at the bottom and pull it from the front toward the back over the peg (illustration 2).

Continue in this manner until I-cord has reached desired length. Secure end by pulling yarn tail through all four stitches.

Tip: A hand-cranked I-cord mill produces I-cord in a wink and comes with detailed instructions.

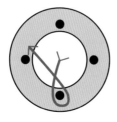

1

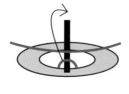

2

Bead Embroidery

Materials

- Tear-proof thread
- Beads
- Beading needle
- Backing paper, masking tape, or paper medical tape to secure edges (optional)
- Embroidery frame (optional)

Knotting Beads

Knotting beads individually in this manner is time-consuming, but well worth the effort because it secures the beads and helps line them up evenly.

Start by pushing the threaded needle up through the fabric from the WS and through the hole in the bead.

Insert the needle straight down through the fabric from the RS, slightly staggered from the initial point.

Directly in the initial point, stitch up through the fabric again from the WS.

With the bead hole pointing sideways, wind the thread around the needle as for a French knot, then reinsert the needle into the fabric in the same spot.

Bead Flower

First, sew on the center bead twice and secure it by knotting as described above.

Now, wrap the thread several times around the thread between the bead and the fabric to create a "base" for the bead.

Thread 6 beads, wrap them around the shank you created, run your thread through all 6 beads again for reinforcement, pull tight and sew in tail.

Bead Cluster

For each stitch, thread 2 to 4 beads onto your needle and sew them on tightly spaced (but not so tightly that they buckle).

Threading Beads for Knitting and Crocheting

Reinforce the beginning tail with liquid glue to create a "needle" that can be used to thread beads directly.

Knitting

Casting On

There are many different ways to cast on. The easiest one is the backward loop cast on: Make a slipknot, slip the knot onto a knitting needle, pull it snug, and hold the needle with the knot in your right hand. Drape the working yarn from the right needle clockwise over your left thumb and hold the end attached to the yarn ball with the last three fingers of your left hand. With the right needle, take up the working yarn from the front, thus forming another loop around the right needle. Pull this loop tight and repeat until you've cast on the required number of sts.

Knit Stitch (k)

When forming a knit stitch, hold the needle with the stitches in your left hand while the working yarn lies behind the needle. Insert the tip of the right needle from the front into the first stitch on the left needle and pull the working yarn back through the first loop toward you, then let the old stitch slide off the left needle.

Purl Stitch (p)

When purling a stitch, the working yarn is in front of the needle. Insert the right needle from the back into the first stitch on the left needle, drape the working yarn from the front to the back around the needle and pull it toward the back through the stitch.

Yarn Over (yo)

To make a yarn over, before knitting or purling the next stitch, place the working yarn around the right needle from the front to the back. Now, work the next stitch. You have increased one stitch.

Knit 2 Together (k2tog)

Right-leaning single decrease: Insert the right needle as if to knit into the second and first stitches on the left needle at the same time. Now, knit both stitches together and let them slide off the left needle. You have decreased one stitch.

Slip 1, Knit 1, Pass Slipped Stitch Over (skp)

Left-leaning single decrease: Slip the first stitch on the left needle knitwise and knit the second stitch. Now, pull the slipped stitch over the knitted one. You have decreased one stitch.

Slip 1, Knit 2 Together, Pass Slipped Stitch Over (sk2p)

Left-leaning double decrease: Slip the first stitch on the left needle knit-wise, then knit the second stitch and the third stitch together. Now, pull the slipped stitch over the two knit together.

Selvedge Stitches (selv st) •

Selvedge stitches are worked to achieve a neat-looking edge. Unless otherwise directed in the patterns, always slip the last stitch of the row. Turn your work and now knit the stitch just slipped through the back loop. Selvedge sts are always knit through the back loop, no matter whether followed by a knit or purl stitch.

Purl 2 Together (p2tog)

Single purled decrease: Insert the right needle into the first and second stitch on the left needle as if to purl and purl them together. You have decreased one stitch.

Purl 3 Together (p3tog)

Double purled decrease: Insert the right needle into the first, second, and third stitches on the left needle as if to purl and purl them together. You have decreased two stitches.

Knit 1 Through the Back Loop (k1-tbl)

Insert the right needle from right to left into the back of the first stitch on the left needle and pull the working yarn through. You have twisted the stitch below the newly formed stitch.

Make 3 from 1 ([k1, yo, k1] into the same st)

Knit the first stitch, but leave it on the left needle. Now, make a yarn over and knit the same first stitch again, then let it slide off the left needle. You have increased two stitches.

Make 1 (M1)

This invisible increase creates a new stitch from the bar between two existing stitches. With your right needle, lift the strand between the stitch just worked and the next stitch on the left-hand needle from the back, place it onto the left needle and knit this stitch through the back loop.

Make 1 Purl Through the Back Loop (M1p-tbl)

Pick up the bar between the stitches on either needle from front to back with the left-hand needle and purl it through the back loop (insert right needle into the stitch from back to front to purl through the back loop).

Slip 1, Knit 3, Pass Slipped Stitch Over (sk3p)

Slip the first stitch from the left needle, knit the next three stitches. Now, pull the slipped stitch over the three knitted stitches.

Binding Off Stitches (BO)

To finish off knitting, the stitches of the last row have to be bound off. Work two sts in pattern onto the right needle. Now, pull the right (first) stitch on the right needle over the left (second) stitch so that only one stitch is on the right needle. Work the next stitch so that there are again two stitches on the right needle, and again pull the right stitch over the left one. Repeat this to the end of the row, until one stitch remains on the right needle. Cut the yarn and pull the tail through this last stitch to secure.

Basic Stitch Patterns

Garter Stitch

In garter stitch, you knit all stitches on both the right side and the wrong side of the fabric. On the right side of the fabric, you will see alternating knit and purl rows.

Stockinette Stitch

With stockinette stitch, you knit all stitches in right side rows and purl all stitches in wrong side rows. On the right side of the fabric, you will see only knit rows.

Ribbing

In ribbing, you alternate between knit and purl stitches in one row. The most common rib pattern is the 2x2 rib: [k2, p2] to the end of the row. Remember what your last two stitches were. If they were purl, start the next row with 2 knit sts; if they were knit, start the next row with 2 purl sts. On the right side of the fabric, you will see vertical columns of knit and purl stitches.

Crocheting

For a neat appearance of the finished item, it is very important to work with even tension throughout.

Chain (ch)

Chains are the foundation of many crocheted items. Every chain starts with a slipknot. Insert the crochet hook into the center of the slipknot, grasp the working yarn with your hook and pull it toward you through the slipknot (illustration 1).

Slip Stitch (sl-st)

Insert the hook through the corresponding stitch of the previous row (or as instructed in the pattern), grasp the working yarn and pull it through toward you. Pull it right away through the loop on the hook (without making an additional yarn over); there is now only one loop on the hook (illustration 2).

Single Crochet (sc)

Insert the hook through the corresponding stitch of the previous row (or as instructed in the pattern), grasp the working yarn (yarn over) and pull it through toward you. Now, yarn over again, hook the working yarn, and pull it through both loops on the hook so you now have one loop on the hook (illustrations 3 and 4).

Front Post Single Crochet (fpsc)

Keeping hook in front of work, insert hook from right to left around post of previous row stitch, grasp the working yarn to create a yarn over, draw up a loop, yarn over, pull working yarn through both loops on hook.

Half Double Crochet (hdc)

Make a yarn over and insert the hook through the previous row stitch. Yarn over again and pull it through toward you—you have three loops on the hook. Make another yarn over and pull it through all three loops; there is now only one loop on the hook (illustrations 5–7).

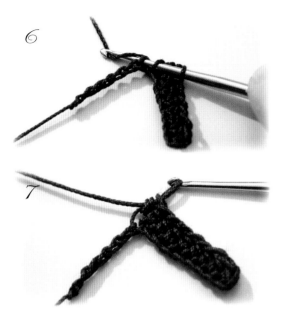

Double Crochet [dc]

Make a yarn over and insert the hook through the previous row stitch. Grasp the working yarn again to create another yarn over and pull it through toward you—you have three loops on the hook. Make another yarn over and pull it through two of the three loops—two loops left on the hook. Make another yarn over and pull it through both loops—only one loop on the hook now (illustrations 8–11).

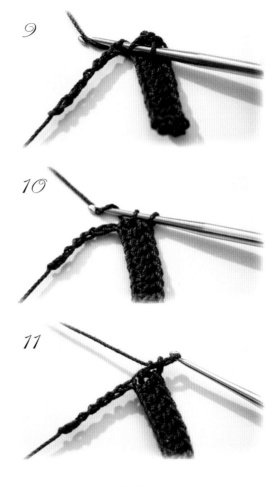

Treble Crochet [tr]

A treble crochet is worked similar to a double crochet (see above); the difference is that at the beginning, instead of one yarn over, you make two yarn overs onto the hook before you insert the hook through the previous row stitch. After you have pulled the working yarn through, there will be four loops on the hook. Grasp the working yarn again and pull it through two of the fours loops on the hook. Now, grasp the working yarn again and pull it through two loops, and a last time, grasp the working yarn again and pull it through both loops.

Three-Dimensional Crocheted Flowers

Materials

- Pearl crochet thread and US 7 (1.5 mm) crochet hook
- Or #1 super fine weight yarn and US B-1 or C-2 (2.5 mm) crochet hook

Special Stitches

- **Front post single crochet (fpsc):** Keeping hook in front of work, insert hook from right to left around post of previous row stitch, grasp the working yarn to create a yarn over, draw up a loop, yarn over, pull working yarn through both loops on hook.
- **Treble crochet 2 together (tr2-tog):** To tr2-tog, work 1 treble crochet, but leave two loops on the hook—don't pull the last loop through yet. Now, work another treble crochet and pull the working yarn through the last 4 loops at once—you have worked a tr2-tog decrease. These decreases will form the calyx.

- **Treble crochet 3 together (tr3-tog):** To tr3-tog, work 1 treble crochet, but leave two loops on the hook—don't pull the last loop through yet. Now, work another treble crochet, leaving 3 total loops on the hook. Work another treble crochet, pulling the working yarn through the last 4 loops at once—you have worked a tr3-tog decrease.

For crisp and firm flowers, work somewhat tightly.

Ch5 and join into round with a sl-st.

Round 1: Ch3, tr1, then [tr2-tog] 4 times.

Round 2: Mount five [sc1, ch4] arcs onto the stitches of the previous round. Close the last arc with a slip stitch.

Round 3: For the first petal row, work [sl-st 1, ch3, tr2-tog, ch3, sl-st 1] into the arcs.

Round 4: For the second petal row, work into Round 1 five [sc1, ch6] arcs, again closing up the last arc with a slip stitch.

Round 5: For the third petal row, work into the arcs: [sl-st 1, ch4, tr3-tog, ch4, sl-st 1].

Weave in all ends.

For the stem, work a chain of the desired length and slip-stitch back over it for reinforcement.

Thread the stem through the center of the flower and either sew the end closed (if adding beads), or knot it.

⬭	chain (ch)
✕	single crochet (sc)
●	slip stitch (sl-st)
✕↓	front post single crochet (fpsc)
⋔	treble crochet 2 together (tr2-tog)
⋔	treble crochet 3 together (tr3-tog)

Decorative Rolls

Materials

- Cotton fabric
- Bondaweb® or other iron-on fabric adhesive on paper carrier
- Sewing thread
- Straight pins
- Embroidery needle
- Fabric scissors
- Ruler
- Iron
- Rotary cutter and cutting mat (optional)
- Ribbons (optional)

Prepare a strip of fabric twice as wide as the desired width of the finished roll. Cut the fabric on the grain, preferably with a rotary cutter on a cutting mat.

Fold the long sides of the prepared fabric strip toward the middle (as you would for double-fold bias tape), and iron it well.

Open up the strip, place a narrow strip Bondaweb® inside, close the strip again and iron over. This will make rolling much easier.

Position the material to be wrapped on the prepared fabric strip and start rolling it tightly.

When the desired thickness has been reached, cut off the excess fabric from the strip, fold the end over toward the inside and pin in place. If desired, add in woven jacquard ribbon or decorative ribbon with the last winding.

Seam using decorative stitches.

Originally published in Germany as *Strickromantik* by Acufactum Ute
Menze

Copyright © 2014 by Acufactum Ute Menze

This translation of *Strickromantik* by Acufactum Ute Menze is
published by arrangement with Silke Bruenink Agency, Munich,
Germany.

This edition copyright © 2015 by Stackpole Books

Published by
STACKPOLE BOOKS
5067 Ritter Road
Mechanicsburg, PA 17055
www.stackpolebooks.com

Design and script, styling and photography: Eva-Maria Maier
Idea and conception: Meike Menze-Stöter
Layout and typesetting: Acufactum, Iserlohn, Stackpole Books
Cover design: Wendy Reynolds
Translation: Katharina Sokiran

Printed in the United States of America

10 9 8 7 6 5 4 3 2 1

First edition

Library of Congress Cataloging-in-Publication Data
Maier, Eva-Maria, 1965–
 [Strickromantik. English]
 Lovely lacy knits : beautiful projects embellished with ribbon,
flowers, beads, and more / Eva-Maria Maier. — First edition.
    pages cm
 Includes bibliographical references and index.
 ISBN 978-0-8117-1479-2 (alk. paper)
1. Needlepoint lace—Patterns. I. Title.
 TT805.N43M3513 2015
 746.44'2—dc23
                    2014037751